ANIMAL FAMILIES
Dolphins

General Editor
Tim Harris

WAYLAND

WAYLAND

This edition published in 2014 by Wayland

Copyright © 2014 Brown Bear Books Ltd.

Wayland
Hachette Children's Books
338 Euston Road
London NW1 3BH

Wayland Australia
Level 17/207 Kent Street
Sydney, NSW 2000

Brown Bear Books Ltd.
First Floor
9–17 St. Albans Place
London
N1 0NX

Managing Editor: Tim Harris
Designer: Lynne Lennon
Picture Manager: Sophie Mortimer
Art Director: Jeni Child
Production Director: Alastair Gourlay
Editorial Director: Lindsey Lowe
Children's Publisher: Anne O'Daly

ISBN: 978-0-7502-8451-6

Printed in China

10 9 8 7 6 5 4 3 2 1

Wayland is a division of Hachette Children's Books,
an Hachette UK company.
www.hachette.co.uk

Websites
The website addresses (URLs) included in this book were valid at the time of going to press. However, because of the nature of the internet, it is possible that some addresses may have changed, or sites may have changed or closed down since publication. While the author and publisher regret any inconvenience this may cause the readers, no responsibility for any such changes can be accepted by either the author or the publisher.

Picture Credits
Key: t = top
Front Cover: Shutterstock: Elena Larina, main; Steve Noakes; tr.
Interior: Corbis: STR/Pakistan/Reuters 27; **FLPA:** Colin Marshall 12/13, Hiroya Minakuchi/Minden Pictures 19; **iStockphoto:** Marcelo Zippo 22; **Shutterstock:** Willyam Bradberry 4, 5, 17, Figen Ciftci 7, Bobby Deal/Real Seal Photos 25, Event 5 6, Guentermanaus 28, Heymo 11, Volodynyr Krasyuk 1, 10, Dale Mitchell 15, Sergey Popov V 9t, Mike Price 29, Anna Sergeren 18, Nickolay Stanev 20, Ugpotulfss 12, Mogens Trolle 23; **Thinkstock:** Hemera 24, iStockphoto 8/9, 16, 26, Stockbyte 21.

Brown Bear Books Ltd. has made every effort to trace copyright holders of the pictures used in this book. Anyone having claims to ownership not identified above is invited to contact smortimer@windmillbooks.co.uk

Contents

Introduction 4

Streamlined swimmers 6

Living in schools 8

Dolphins living together 10

Expert fishers 12

Helping each other 14

Mating dolphins 16

Caring for the young 18

Places where dolphins live 20

Close relations 22

Echolocation 24

Dolphins in rivers 26

Captive dolphins 28

Glossary 30

Further reading 31

Index 32

Introduction

Of the many creatures that live in the sea, dolphins are among the best known. There are lots of things about dolphins that will surprise you, though.

Dolphins are mammals. All mammals are warm-blooded, or endothermic, animals. That means they can keep their bodies at a steady temperature. Like you and me, dolphins have a bony skeleton and breathe air. Dolphin babies drink their mother's milk. Dolphins love to mix with other

Some dolphins love riding on waves, as surfers do. This may help them save energy, but they probably also do it just for fun.

dolphins. Many live in groups of several thousand.

Dolphins spend most of their lives in the water. In the same way that submarines navigate using sonar, dolphins use sound to 'map' their surroundings and hunt with great accuracy. This ability is called echolocation.

Dolphins at work

The U.S. Navy uses dolphins to find explosive mines, search for people lost at sea and to carry tools to underwater sites. The U.S. Navy's Marine Mammal Program was set up to study how dolphins can swim so fast. The navy wanted to use this information to improve submarine, torpedo and ship designs. It soon realised that dolphins had many other useful skills.

Dolphins are very inquisitive. They always want to know what is happening around them.

Dolphins at play

In the ocean dolphins often leap high out of the water. They sometimes catch jellyfish and then use their tails to toss them into the air like a ball. Spinner dolphins leap out of the water and spin right around like a top.

Streamlined swimmers

There are more than 30 different species (types) of dolphins, and they all look different. There are spotted dolphins and striped dolphins.

Some dolphins are black and white, others are blue and a few are pink. They vary greatly in length, ranging from 1.2 metres (4 ft) to more than 4 metres (13 ft). All dolphins have sleek, streamlined bodies. They also have powerful tails divided into two lobes, or flukes. Most dolphins have a fin on the back that helps keep them from rolling over as they swim. On each side of the body, behind the head, is a flipper. Dolphins use their flippers to steer.

The blowhole

Most dolphins have a snout, or beak. Dolphins cannot breathe through their mouths like us – that way only leads to the stomach. Instead, they breathe through a hole on the top of

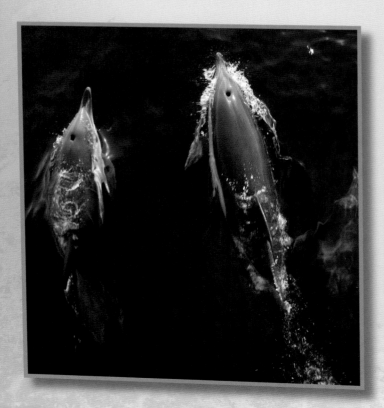

Dolphins breathe through the blowhole on top of the head. These are bottlenose dolphins.

their head called the blowhole. This hole allows the dolphin to take a quick breath when it comes to the surface. The blowhole closes when the dolphin is underwater so it does not drown.

Dolphins have a thick layer of fat called blubber. This keeps their body warm. When they are very active, dolphins can overheat. To cool down, more warm blood flows around the fins and flippers, letting heat escape into the water. To warm the animal up, less blood flows through these parts.

Fast swimmers

Some dolphins reach speeds of more than 40 kilometres per hour (25 mph). A dolphin's tail beats up and down to propel the animal forwards. It has no features that would disturb the smooth flow of water over the body, such as ear flaps, legs or hair. The smooth body shape helps the animal move quickly through water.

Each of these dolphins has a fin on its back. This is called the dorsal fin.

Living in schools

Most dolphins live with other dolphins in groups called schools, or pods. Ocean-living dolphins team up in the biggest schools.

Coastal dolphins usually live in smaller groups, and river dolphins mostly hang out alone or in pairs. Big schools of ocean-living dolphins often contain groups of mothers and their babies, as well as groups of young dolphins. Adult males usually swim around alone or with one or two other males.

Adult males

Striped dolphins do things differently. Groups of juveniles, mating adults and non-mating adults team up to form a school.

◉ **A large school of common dolphins in the Sea of Cortez, Mexico. They are all swimming in the same direction.**

This tightly packed group of white-sided dolphins is swimming underwater.

That means there is less separation between the males and the females than there is in other species.

Coming and going

The members of one of the small groups usually stay the same, but the make-up of a large dolphin school changes as groups come and go. For example, a group of grown-up males may stay away from the school for months at a time.

Watching for enemies

A dolphin school may contain several species. In the Pacific Ocean groups of spotted dolphins play, rest and mate during the day and feed at night. Spinner dolphins in the same waters rest at night and feed in the day, so there are always some dolphins on the lookout for predators.

Dolphins living together

Why do dolphins live in groups? They rely on each other's help to find food and watch for predators. Females help each other to raise the babies.

In the vast oceans, the large shoals of fish that dolphins seek out to eat can be far apart. So, being part of a group makes it easier for a dolphin to find food.

Perhaps most importantly, living in a group gives protection. Dolphins have few enemies, but those they do have are fearsome: sharks and killer whales. A lone dolphin would be no match for a large shark, but several dolphins together can chase a shark

These two bottlenose dolphins are showing affection by touching their snouts together.

White-sided dolphins blow bubbles to warn other dolphins of danger.

away. They do this by butting and ramming the shark.

Squeaks and whistles

Dolphins 'talk' to each other using squeaks, whistles and groans. Bottlenose dolphins have signature whistles. Like a name, each animal has its own sound.

Dolphins also use body language. Leaping clear out of the water tells other dolphins that there are fish to hunt, sharks to avoid, or dolphins in distress. An angry dolphin claps its jaws together, rams with its head, or smacks with its tail. Dolphins like to pet their friends, though, and they use their head or mouth to stroke other dolphins.

Getting some shuteye

Dolphins need to rest, but the ocean is a dangerous place. A fast-moving shark can easily catch a sleeping dolphin. Dolphins have solved this problem by living in groups and letting only half their brain sleep at any one time. This means they can take turns sleeping.

Expert fishers

Dolphins are fast-swimming hunters, mainly of fish, squid and octopus. Prey is swallowed whole, head first.

Dolphins hunt for their food in different ways. Those living in shallow waters take fish off the seafloor. Common dolphins swim underneath a fish, driving it out of the water, and then leap up to snatch it out of the air. Indo-Pacific humpback dolphins wriggle across mudbanks to catch their lunch.

Fish bait

Around coral reefs and rocky coasts a dolphin might catch a fish, then use it as bait to tempt other fish hiding in crevices. Dolphins may use very high-pitched clicks to stun their prey. All dolphins have teeth; but their size and number vary according to diet. Some dolphins have only a few teeth; others have more than 100. Risso's dolphins, which eat mainly soft squid and octopus, have only a few teeth at the front of their mouth, and none on the top jaw.

↺ **Bottlenose dolphins have between 72 and 104 teeth for grasping slippery fish.**

Cooperative feeding

Coastal dolphins, and those that live in rivers, hunt alone or in pairs. Deep-ocean dolphins hunt together. A group will herd the fish together, then take turns at swimming through the shoal and eating. Some slap the fish with their tail to stun them. Commerson's dolphins form a half-circle and herd the fish against the shore before lunching.

⬆ These long-beaked common dolphins have herded together a large shoal of fish. Now the dolphins will swim through the shoal again and again, eating until they have had enough.

Helping each other

Dolphins help protect each other. If a dusky dolphin screeches in a certain way, for example, the others in its group know that a killer whale is in the area.

If a dolphin does come to harm, though, its companions will come to the rescue. Several dolphins will use their snouts or backs to keep the injured dolphin afloat. They will also make sure its blowhole is out of the water so it can breathe. When members of a dolphin group swim ashore and get stuck, other dolphins will risk their lives trying to help their friends.

There have even been reports of dolphins protecting people from sharks. The dolphins swam in circles around the people until the sharks went away.

The dolphin in the centre has been injured, and its two friends are nudging it back to the surface.

Why do dolphins get stuck?

It is not clear why dolphins sometimes become stuck on beaches. They have tiny crystals of magnetite, a magnetic mineral, inside their heads. Dolphins probably use the crystals like compasses for reading Earth's magnetic field. Maybe sometimes the 'compass' makes a mistake, so the dolphins swim ashore, not out to sea.

A white-beaked dolphin has become stranded on a beach.

However, dolphins are not always protective towards other dolphins. Dead baby dolphins have been found with wounds inflicted by adult dolphins. It could be that male dolphins kill the young of certain females so that those females will mate with them. Perhaps females even kill their own young if food is scarce.

Much to learn

Maybe, just like people, dolphins are unselfish when it suits them. However, under difficult circumstances, for example when food is short, they have to behave differently to survive. We still have much to learn about dolphin behaviour and society.

Mating dolphins

Male dolphins are called bulls, and female dolphins are called cows. It can be hard for people to tell them apart, just by looking.

Males tend to be larger than females, but this is not always the case. Male Amazon river dolphins are a little longer and much heavier than females. They are also pinker than the females. Male and female bottlenose dolphins are very similar in size, shape and colour. Male bottlenose dolphins are ready to breed from 10 to 12 years old. The females can breed at a much younger age – usually between 5 and 12 years old. In some species the size of a dolphin is more important than its age in deciding when it is able to mate.

Fighting males

Most dolphins breed at particular times of the year. Bottlenose dolphins breed between spring and autumn. During the mating season males fight over females and chase each other at top speed, showing off to the females. Sometimes males are scarred as a result of these fights.

Two spinner dolphins perform an underwater display before they mate.

Female dolphins are pregnant for about a year. The babies, or calves, are born tail first. Twins and triplets are very rare but are sometimes born.

Kidnappers

During the mating season, male bottlenose dolphins may work together to 'kidnap' a female away from her group. They take turns at feeding as the others guard her from other males. The female may be held captive for weeks. The males do this so they can be sure of fathering offspring.

A small group of bottlenose dolphins plays together underwater. It is very hard to tell which are male and which female.

Helping out

Giving birth is a risky business for the mother and calf. Sharks are attracted by blood, so the mother needs other dolphins to protect her. Pregnant bottlenose dolphins often give birth with a couple of other females swimming nearby.

Caring for the young

For at least the first year of its life, a bottlenose dolphin will stay with its mother in a dolphin nursery. A nursery has several adult females.

The adult females have a lot to teach the young about how to survive at sea. The young learn how to hunt, echolocate and mix with other dolphins. The fathers have little to do with their children, but there are many other females around who share the task of looking after the young. In a large group of dolphins

A spinner dolphin calf swims with its mother in the Red Sea, Egypt.

the nursery will travel in the middle, surrounded by other dolphins. There, the calves are safe from predators.

Bonds that last

After one to two years the calf may leave the nursery and start hanging out with other dolphins of a similar age. When they are older, females will return to the nursery as adults. The young males form their own groups.

Even when they are fully grown, dolphins often remain in touch with their mothers. Many return to visit mum after the birth of a brother or sister. Dolphins also seem to form bonds with those they grew up with in the nursery.

A Commerson's dolphin calf suckles from its mother. This calf is a few months old. By the time it is one year old, it will be almost as long as its mother.

Nursing babies

A baby dolphin feeds on its mother's milk. The milk is much richer than human milk, and this helps the baby grow quickly. The calf cannot suck, so the mother squirts milk into its mouth. A young bottlenose dolphin is suckled for at least a year.

Places where dolphins live

Dolphins live in all the world's oceans and in some large rivers. They are more common in warm tropical waters than in the coldest oceans.

Some dolphins live around coral reefs, which are found only in warm waters less than 30 metres (100 ft) deep. Clymene dolphins and rough-toothed dolphins are found in much deeper waters. Not all dolphins are sea creatures. Some live only in rivers, such as the Amazon in Brazil and the Ganges in India. Others can live in fresh or salty water.

Hector's dolphins live only in shallow ocean waters, less than 100 metres (330 ft) deep, around New Zealand.

↩ **This striped dolphin has been caught in a drift net in the Atlantic Ocean. It will drown if it is not rescued. Trawlers use drift nets to catch large numbers of fish.**

Threatened habitats

Some dolphins swim in every ocean, but others live in much smaller areas. Coasts and rivers are becoming more built up. Often that means there is more water pollution. Dolphins that only live in a small area are more at risk from habitat loss, pollution and fishing nets.

Many more dolphins range the open seas, often far from land. They swim and feed in the well-lit surface waters, some diving down to darker waters to hunt.

Muddy waters

The type of place, or habitat, a dolphin lives in can affect what the dolphin looks like. Coastal bottlenose dolphins tend to be smaller than ocean-living ones. The reasons for this are not known, but the differences can be so great that some experts think they are separate species. Compared to their marine relatives, river dolphins have very poor eyesight. Good eyesight would be wasted in the muddy waters they swim in.

Close relations

Dolphins belong to the group of mammals called cetaceans. 'Cetacean' is the ancient Greek word for sea monster. Whales are also cetaceans.

One whale, the blue whale, is the largest animal on Earth. Cetaceans spend all their lives in water, unlike other sea-living mammals such as seals. Seals haul themselves out of the water to breed and raise their young.

The cetaceans include two groups of living whales: baleen whales and toothed whales. Baleen whales are the giants of the oceans. They have no teeth, but large plates of baleen hang down

The humpback whale is a giant baleen whale. It grows to 19 metres (62 ft) in length and can live for 100 years.

⟳ Killer whales, or orcas, can grow up to 10 metres (32 feet) long. As their name suggests, they are aggressive hunters.

from their upper jaw. Baleen is made from the same material as fingernails.

Toothed whales have teeth and are able to echolocate. All marine dolphins are actually small toothed whales.

Dolphin ancestors

The ancestors of modern dolphins lived on land. They had fur, four legs and no flippers. Over millions of years these early mammals evolved (changed gradually) into cetaceans. Perhaps the changes began when the land mammals started to feed on fish in coastal waters. They began to live a more and more aquatic lifestyle until they abandoned land altogether.

Dolphin names

The term dolphin refers to any member of the family Delphinidae (oceanic dolphins) or family Platanistidae (river dolphins). Usually, it is the smaller oceanic dolphins that are called dolphins. The larger ones are called whales. Orcas, or killer whales, are the largest oceanic dolphins. Because of their large size, they are usually called whales.

Echolocation

When we look at something, we are seeing reflected light. In a similar way dolphins can 'see' objects by picking up reflected sound with their ears.

This is called echolocation. The dolphin sends out a series of clicks, often too high-pitched for humans to hear. The sound waves bounce off objects in the water. The dolphin listens to the returning echoes of the clicks and uses this information to picture its surroundings.

When a dolphin is hunting a fish, it sweeps the beam of sound over the animal by moving its head from side to side. As the dolphin gets nearer to its prey, the clicks get closer together and become much higher pitched.

⬇ **Without the ability to echolocate, these leaping dolphins would not be able to find fish and feed.**

A dolphin's melon gives its head a distinctive shape. For the dolphin this is far more important than just good looks.

The dolphin can see more with sound than we can with light. That is because the echoes reveal the inside of things as well as their shape and size.

Hearing

Dolphins have no earflaps, but their sense of hearing is very good. They have a tiny hole that leads to a sensitive inner ear. However, most sounds reach the inner ear by passing through the blubber of the lower jaw, not this hole. Sound travels faster through water than air, and dolphins can hear sounds coming from several kilometres away.

How a dolphin's melon and inner ear help it track and catch fish.

The melon

The forehead of a dolphin generally bulges over the beak. This part of the head contains a fatty, oily organ called the melon. The melon acts like the lens of a camera, focusing the clicks into a powerful beam that can travel for up to 800 metres (2,600 ft). Another fat store in the lower jaw helps channel the returning echoes to the ear.

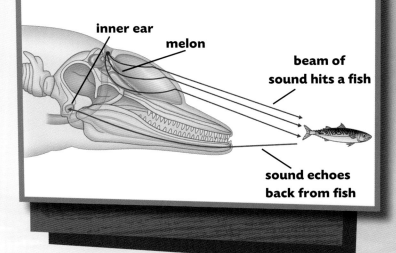

inner ear

melon

beam of sound hits a fish

sound echoes back from fish

Dolphins in rivers

Not all dolphin species live in the oceans. Some of the largest rivers in the world are home to dolphins found nowhere else on Earth.

The River Ganges in India and the River Indus in Pakistan are home to the South Asian river dolphin. The boto, or Amazon river dolphin, lives in several rivers in South America. It is the biggest of the river dolphins, growing to 2.5 metres (8 ft) long. River dolphins are among the rarer and most interesting of dolphins. They feed on fish, crabs, turtles and shrimps caught in their long, pointed jaws, which are stocked with more than 100 teeth. River dolphins are particularly good at echolocating. They have to be, since the waters where they live are often dark and muddy. It is sometimes impossible for the dolphins to see beyond the end of their beak.

Endangered species

River dolphins are at risk all over the world. River dolphins normally migrate upriver in the rainy season. Dams, such as the Three Gorges Dam (right) on the River Yangtze in China, keep them from doing this in some rivers. This is one reason why the baiji river dolphin of the River Yangtze is now extinct.

The river dolphins of the Ganges and Indus are almost blind. They rely on echolocation and probing the river bottom with their snouts to find food.

Small groups

River dolphins live in smaller groups than their ocean-living cousins. South Asian river dolphins live in pairs or alone. Amazon river dolphins swim in small family groups. With few natural predators (apart from people), river dolphins do not really need to live in large groups as marine dolphins do. Like marine dolphins, though, the mothers still take good care of their young.

People prepare to carry out a health check on an endangered South Asian river dolphin from the River Indus in Pakistan.

Captive dolphins

Keeping dolphins in captivity allows people to see these beautiful animals in the flesh. It can also make people think about how to protect them.

Well-known and well-loved animals are more likely to gain the attention that can make governments protect them in the wild. If numbers of wild dolphins go down, it might be possible to use captive dolphins to restock the oceans. Keeping dolphins in captivity has also allowed scientists to study them closely. Scientists can use their knowledge to advise on how best to protect wild dolphins.

Life in a dolphinarium

Some dolphinariums (places where dolphins are kept in captivity) treat their dolphins well. Others do more harm than good, though. Not all dolphinariums tell their visitors how to respect the dolphins. Sometimes, captive dolphins are released back into the wild. If a release is carried out in the right way, the dolphins are taken back to where they were first captured. If all goes well, the released dolphins will be accepted into a local group of wild dolphins.

⟲ **A captive Amazon river dolphin, a species that is endangered in the wild. Dolphins bred in captivity may one day help boost numbers in the wild.**

Training dolphins

People train dolphins by praising the behaviour they want to see and ignoring things they do not want to see. As soon as the dolphin does something right, the trainer will blow a whistle or say 'Good'. The trainer will then do something the dolphin likes: feeding it a fish, rubbing it down or playing with it.

Dolphins are intelligent animals and can be taught many tricks in captivity. These bottlenose dolphins are leaping over a rope.

29

Glossary

ancestors Animals from which dolphins have developed over many generations.

baleen whale Kind of whale with a fringe-like sieve along its upper jaw. The sieve traps krill from the water.

blowhole The nostril opening on a dolphin or whale's head that allows the animal to breathe.

blubber Layer of fat under a dolphin's skin that keeps the animal warm.

breach Leap clear of the water.

calf Baby dolphin that is still being nursed by its mother.

cetacean One of a group of water-living mammals including dolphins, whales and porpoises.

dorsal fin Fin on the back of a dolphin.

echolocation System used by dolphins to find their way and find food. Dolphins echolocate by making loud noises and then 'reading' the returning echoes.

flukes The lobes on a dolphin's tail.

krill Tiny shrimp-like animals that live in ocean waters.

mammal A kind of animal that is warm-blooded and has a backbone. Female mammals have glands that produce milk to feed their young.

melon The organ on a dolphin's head that focuses the animal's clicking sounds into a powerful beam to echolocate.

migration Regular movement of animals from one region to another.

nursery A group of female dolphins and their young.

predator An animal that hunts and kills other animals for food.

Further Reading

Books

Animal Instincts: A Curious Dolphin. Tom Jackson. London: Hachette Children's Books, 2013.

Everything Dolphins: All the Dolphin Facts, Photos, and Fun that will Make You Flip. Elizabeth Carney. Washington, D.C.: National Geographic, 2012.

Freshwater Giants: Hippopotamuses, River Dolphins and Manatees. Phyllis Perry. London: Franklin Watts, 2000.

Mammal (Eyewitness). Steve Parker. London: Natural History Museum, 2003.

Whales and Dolphins. Susannah Davidson. London: Usborne, 2008.

World of Animals. Susannah Davidson. London: Usborne, 2013.

Websites

Worldwide Fund for Nature
There are several pages on dolphins, porpoises and whales.
www.wwf.org.uk/Dolphins

American Cetacean Society
Conservation news from the world's first cetacean protection organisation.
www.acsonline.org

Facts About Dolphins
Top facts about lots of dolphin species.
www.dolphins-world.com

Learn About Dolphins
Games and activities that give insights into the fascinating lives of dolphins and whales.
www.wdcs.org/wdcskids/en/interactive.php

Index

Amazon River 20
Amazon river dolphin 16, 26, 27, 28

baiji river dolphin 26
baleen 22–23
baleen whales 22
beak 6
blowhole 6, 7, 14
blubber 7, 25
blue whale 22
boto 26
bottlenose dolphin 6, 10, 11, 12, 16, 17, 18–19, 21, 29
brain 11
breathing 6

captivity 28–29
cetaceans 22, 23
clymene dolphin 20
Commerson's dolphin 13, 19
common dolphin 8, 12, 13

dams 26
dolphinarium 28
drowning 7, 21
dusky dolphin 14

ears 24–25
echolocation 5, 18, 24–25, 26, 27
endothermic (warm-blooded) animals 4
eyesight 21

fat 7, 25
female dolphins 8–9, 10, 15, 16–17, 18–19
fin 6, 7
fish 10, 11, 12, 13, 23, 24, 25, 26, 29
fishing nets 21
flipper 6, 7, 23
fluke 6

Ganges River 20, 26–27

Hector's dolphin 20
herding 13
humpback whale 22
hunting 13, 18, 23

India 20, 26
Indus River 26–27

jaws 11, 12, 23, 25

kidnapping 17
killer whale, or orca 10, 14, 23

male dolphin 8–9, 15, 16–17, 19
mammals 4, 23
mating 15, 16–17
melon 25
milk 4, 19

nursery 18, 19

Pakistan 26, 27

playing 17
pollution 21
predators 9, 10, 19, 27
pregnant 17

Risso's dolphin 12
river dolphins 23, 26–27
rough-toothed dolphin 20

school 8–9
sharks 10, 11, 14, 17
sonar 5
South Asian river dolphin 26, 27
spinner dolphin 5, 9, 16, 18
spotted dolphin 6, 9
striped dolphin 6, 21
suckling 19

tail 6, 7, 11
teeth 12, 22, 23
toothed whales 23

U.S. Navy 5

whales 22
whistles 11
white-beaked dolphin 15
white-sided dolphin 9, 11

Yangtze River 26